SAILING TO SIMPLICITY

SAILING TO SIMPLICITY

LIFE LESSONS LEARNED AT SEA

Migael Scherer

INTERNATIONAL MARINE / McGRAW-HILL

Camden, Maine • New York • San Francisco • Washington, D.C. • Auckland
Bogotá • Caracas • Lisbon • London • Madrid • Mexico City • Milan • Montreal
New Delhi • San Juan • Singapore • Sydney • Tokyo • Toronto

International Marine

A Division of The **McGraw·Hill** Companies

Permissions for previously published material appear on pages 162–63, which constitute a continuation of the copyright page.

10 9 8 7 6 5 4 3 2 1
Copyright © 2000 International Marine

Library of Congress Cataloging-in-Publication Data
Scherer, Migael.
     Sailing to simplicity : life lessons learned at sea / Migael Scherer.
        p.   cm.
     ISBN 0-07-135326-7
     1. Sailing Anecdotes.   I. Title
   GV811.S355   2000
   797. 1'24—dc21   99-40474
                                                CIP

This book is printed on 55-lb. Sebago

Printed by R. Donnelley & Son, Crawfordsville, IN; Design and illustrations by Dennis Anderson; Production by Archetype, Shannon Thomas, and Dan Kirchoff; Edited by Tom McCarthy and Joanne Allen

Dacron, Pall Mall, and Toll House are registered trademarks.

For my husband, with love.

May the stories continue.

CONTENTS

PREFACE

I generally begin exploring a new subject by reading children's books. They're clear and engaging—a good springboard. When my editor asked me to think about writing a "Zen" approach to sailing, I found something even better: the comic books of Tsai Chih Chung.

These are no ordinary comics. For one thing, the titles are far too lyrical: *Zen Speaks: Shouts of Nothingness, The Dao of Zhuangzi: The Harmony of Nature,* and *The Tao Speaks: Lao-Tzu's Whispers of Wisdom.* For another, the stories—sometimes humorous, always down-to-earth—are too indirect, and though each ends with a simple message or aphorism, simple doesn't mean easy.

All the aphorisms in this book are from these three titles.

I moved on to more conventional books but always returned to Tsai's. What struck me wasn't "enlightenment"—by then it was obvious that I couldn't presume to understand in a few months what requires a lifetime—but rather how learning on the water follows this ancient way of learning: obliquely, through story. There's instruction—all those how-to articles and books—but what we really know, in an immediate and visceral way, we know through experiences that have been distilled through story. The message sheds light on the narrative but doesn't replace it.

As I reflected on these lessons, *Sailing to Simplicity* took shape. Stories surfaced, my own and others', stories shared across cockpits and galley tables. In my twenty-five years afloat I've heard hundreds, and I'm always eager to hear another. Life on a boat—rowing, sailing, or motoring—is a life of change and discovery. Every cruise is a shakedown: things go wrong when we least expect, or right in ways we don't deserve. On every voyage we learn, and learn again.

I hope these stories help readers revive their own.

SETTING OUT

I can still remember how I felt as a kid the first time I pushed away from the beach on a raft. No more than 20 feet out and I was free. The grown-ups who waved from land seemed trapped there, and small. I belonged to a different, liquid world.

Right away that world grabbed my attention. I didn't know the terms *displacement* and *stability*, but when I stood up and the flimsy pallet beneath me teetered, I sat back down again. The narrow board that was my paddle seemed to work in one direction only—in circles—and the laughing water pushed me this way and that, alternately inviting and daring me to go farther.

I got nowhere that day, of course, yet I wasn't discouraged. I was just a kid, captivated with the going.

Now that I'm an adult, with a real boat, I push away from the dock with a destination in mind—as if the water were no more than a road. But as soon as the lines are cast off, I'm reminded that it is not. The sense of escape is immediate and intoxicating. The shore retreats, becomes a smudge of quickly forgotten activity. My attention is focused entirely on the present, on the smoothness or chop of the seas, the sound of the engine or the set of the sails, the suddenly enormous sky. And what's this? A gust of wind sends the bow to starboard, though I'm steering to port. Current tugs at the rudder. Is that a log floating ahead? Could be a tide rip. Sure is, and birds too, everywhere. What are they?

I'm that kid again, learning anew.

*Asking where the road lies is
a great mistake because there
is no road. We have been on
the way all along.*

ANGLE OF HEEL

My god, I'm tipping!

There I was, a grown woman alone in a sailing skiff, ducking my head as the boom swayed to port, to starboard, to port. Alarmed because the boat had heeled over.

My alarm was so visceral that it surprised me. Heeling is necessary in order to go forward against the wind, but the instant the boat tipped I'd released the sheet and the tiller as naturally as I would have pulled my hand back from a hot stove. What I knew about sailing, my body just didn't believe.

I'd brought myself on purpose to the middle of the

lake on this day in the middle of the summer. It hadn't been difficult. I'd simply raised the sail, let out the line until the boom was almost perpendicular to the boat, and held the tiller straight. I'd steered this way and that, pulled the sheet in a bit or let it out, as I'd learned to do the weekend before, when my husband had taken me out for my first lesson. We'd ended up snipping at each other so much that he had finally gotten out of the boat and pushed me off to figure it out myself. I'd ended up rowing back to the dock that day, but at least I was comfortable with how the tiller went one way and the boat the other, and I could use a following breeze.

Today I wanted to *sail* all the way back to the dock, against the wind. Conditions were perfect: a light breeze, warm sun, hardly any chop—just enough to make the water sparkle. Since early spring I'd been watching the sailing races here. Upwind, the boats leaned over, the crews in their cockpits intent but not anxious. They made it look easy and natural, the way a skier who traverses a slope, body swaying, seems to exert no effort at all. And when, once, I'd been invited on one of the boats (I'd done no more than take orders on the main sheet), the heeling hadn't bothered me so much. What made me so nervous about tipping now?

I reminded myself how when going against the wind the sail fills, the pressure pushes it over, and the keel—a daggerboard in this case—resists. But it was like listening to a lecture on gyroscopes while learning to ride a bicycle; the fact is, you might fall, but sooner or later you had to get on and start pedaling. The more I deliberated now, the farther I drifted from my destination.

I centered myself on the bottom of the boat, cross-legged. The worst that could happen was getting wet, which I already was from the shallow puddle beneath me on the floorboards. I pulled the tiller to port, and the nose turned to starboard. The breeze filled the sail, and the boat started to tip as before, but this time I didn't let go of both the sail and the tiller—I only let go of the sail. The boat immediately straightened up and started to slip backward.

OK, that was a little better. Maybe I should try doing the opposite: hold the sail in and let the tiller go. I didn't work out in my head what the result would be, though I was sure this skittish little boat would let me know right away. I sheeted in the boom almost to the gunwale and held it there. The boat heeled at once, but instead of letting go of the tiller, I instinctively leaned in the opposite direction and jerked it with me to starboard. The little boat lurched, then began to move forward at an angle to the wind.

Forward—that was what I wanted! I eased the tiller

a bit more toward me and, wonderfully, picked up more speed. Water slapped the bow, making a happy sound. Sailing now, heeled over, I leaned to the high side. Neither I nor the boat was level, but together we were balanced. The boat no longer felt like it was tipping over; the sensation instead was like lifting—lifting and gliding. And the more I pulled the sail or the tiller toward me, the faster I seemed to go.

Until, sheeting in too far, pulling the tiller too close, the boat and I were aimed straight into the wind, upright, sails flapping uselessly, going nowhere.

To bend is to stay whole;
to tilt is to remain upright.

THE PERFECT AIRFOIL

Concentrate. This is a big boat, with big sails.

"If the telltales are horizontal, the wind passing across the surface of the sail is exactly right. But if so much as one of those little strings begins to droop or wave up and down, then the jib either needs to be brought in or let out."

The reason has something to do with air pressure.

"Keep the most pressure on the inner, windward side of the curve, less on the opposite, so that the air molecules create lift. You know, like an airplane. Think of sawing a cross section of an airplane wing. See the

shape at the slice? That's what you're after in the sail—
a curve like that."

I listen, eyes skyward, and imagine an airplane, crippled for the sake of my edification, careening from the sky. The passengers and crew are doomed.

"Look. See the way the luff is just beginning to break?"

Sure enough, the outer edge of the jib is threatening to fold inward. I nod.

"That's precisely where you want that sail to be. Find that spot, then sheet in a bit. That's where you reach maximum efficiency. Not that much—you're pinching. Either fall off or let the sail out. The center of effort is about three-quarters down, so the thrust . . . "

And my attention wanders.

Years ago, when I taught eighth-grade geography, I'd spoken in that same incredulous, pleading tone. The lesson was time zones. I'd held an orange in one hand and a globe in the other. "See, the orange is the sun, and as the earth turns, daylight strikes it at different times." The students had looked at me as if I were telling them something so obvious that they were insulted, or so preposterous that they doubted my sanity. I then assigned a time zone to each row. "If it's ten o'clock at night in South Carolina, what time is it in Denver?" Their eyes had glassed.

What I should have done was put the entire class on a plane to London. Time would have had dimension then; it would have been something to reckon with, not just move through, like air.

I close my eyes and take a deep breath. The air is salty and sweet. I can feel the wind on my left ear. For no reason that I can explain, I move the wheel a fraction of an inch to starboard.

"That's it! You've got it!"

But the boat, enlivened, has already told me.

Any time we use words to explain

something, there will be deficiencies.

That which is asked about is itself

the most complete answer.

COMING ABOUT

As the crow flies, it's only a mile back to the dock. But I am not a crow, just a sailor in a little pram, beating to windward on a port tack.

The water tickles the hull as it prances along. The breeze flirts with my hair. I kneel on the floorboards, tiller against my chest, and sheet the boom in closer to the gunwale. The daggerboard is all the way down, a blade in the water to hold my course.

Where I am headed right now is not where I really want to go. My destination is over there, at ten o'clock to the bow's twelve o'clock. It's the best I can do with this single battened sail, in this breeze, though to be honest, I probably wouldn't point much higher with another rig. Upwind sailing always requires an oblique approach; you get where you want by going sideways. Way over in one direction, then way over in the other. If going straight is important, drop the sail and row.

Toward shore the water is glassy—there's no breeze there. I duck my head and in one motion shift my body to the other side of the boat, moving the tiller with me. The Dacron quivers and rustles as the bow sweeps past the eye of the wind and the boom swings to port. The sail seems to take a deep breath, then fills, and the little boat is off again.

This is one of those times when coming about feels like an about-face, for I am now sailing, with great enthusiasm, in the wrong direction. More west than north, very nearly southwest. My destination isn't off my starboard beam; it's off my starboard quarter.

Such is beating. Satisfying progress forward, less satisfying but necessary progress backward. Forth and back, port tack and starboard tack, I crisscross the lake. West, then northeast, then west again. There's where I am and where I want to end up, and the course in between absorbs all my happy attention. A cat's-paw darkens a patch of water ahead, and I point higher to meet the stiffened breeze, then fall off the instant it passes. I surf briefly on the wake of a yacht that crosses behind. With each coming about I climb the wind that blows against me.

Advancing is retreating and retreating is advancing; they both arrive and they both depart.

15

TRIMMING THE SAILS

Mizzen, main, jib: upwind it's aftmost sail first.

Hand over hand, I raised the mizzen. The metal cars slid up the track, the Dacron flapped, and I thought of a weather vane, how simple physics keeps *Orca's* bow pointed into the wind. A few ratchets on the winch and I cleated the halyard.

Then the mainsail. Paul was already at the mast, nodding. I nodded back, and as he pulled down on the halyard I took in the slack at the winch as fast as I could. He joined me in the cockpit to winch up the last foot. I turned my full attention to the wheel, to keep

Orca from falling off. I could feel her eagerness beneath my feet, a straining against me through the rudder: she wanted to sail.

Then the jib sang its way up the stainless wire, and *Orca* became more insistent, sails flapping impatiently. I kept the bow into the wind until the jib halyard was taut and secure.

"Topping lift," Paul mouthed from amidships, and I released the line at the mizzen mast as he released the line at the main. The boom seemed to sag downward with relief. I eased the wheel to starboard, Paul eased out the sheets, and the sails filled. *Orca* moved forward.

"Turn us back into the wind for a sec," Paul said. "The main halyard's a little loose." True enough, there was the barest scalloping all along the sail at the mast.

"Now we're ready for some trim." He rubbed his hands together with delight at the prospect of adjusting everything. Jib, then main, then mizzen, each sail angled in just a tad more than the one behind it. He fussed with the main traveler until he was satisfied with the shape of the sail. Then he sheeted all the sails in a bit, frowned at the result, and let them out again. I kept us on course, noting with pleasure how *Orca* indeed picked up speed, not much—the wind was hardly stiff—but enough to create a satisfying wake.

Isn't it strange how the sensation of speed on a sailboat is entirely out of proportion to reality? We couldn't have been going five knots, less than eight miles per hour, yet I was exhilarated as I never am when riding five times as fast in a car. Everything contributes to the feeling—the rush of water, the whoosh of wind, the rise and fall of the hull, the elliptical movement of the masthead against the sky. And everything holds my attention, like the shape of the sail and the pressure on the wheel, the barest turning or softening of the wind against my face. The passing shore. Other boats.

"Look," I said, pointing to a sailboat a quarter-mile off our stern. Ketch rigged with a clipper bow and a low pilothouse, it was a lot like *Orca*, and it seemed to be gaining on us. Suddenly we weren't going very fast at all.

"We could sheet in, get more speed," Paul said. "Point up a bit." He cranked in the main and the jib as I turned the wheel to port. I glanced at the other sailboat—still gaining—and that quickly, *Orca*'s jib began to luff, the trailing edge fluttering into slow S curves. The block on the mainsail boom shifted slightly. Small signs, but in another thirty seconds both sails would backwind, and we would be stalled, in irons.

I turned the wheel back to where it had been. Paul

let out the sails. *Orca* paused a moment, as if making sure she had our attention. Sails full once more, she continued on.

We waved at the other boat as it sailed by.

If your mind becomes
attached to something external
you will lose your
concentration and your skill.

READING THE WEATHER

Morning. A halyard is slapping, "Let's go, let's go." The rigging creaks, "Stay."

First, look out the hatch. What color is the water? Is it pale blue, deep navy, pearl gray, or charcoal? Is the surface rippled, ruffled, flecked with white, dimpled, or polished? What's happening above? Does the sky seem washed with light or scrubbed by wind? Are the clouds high or low, dawdling along or racing by?

Feel the air on your face, feel it cooling or warming.

Now check the barometer. Consider it another sense, delicate as touch. Is the pressure rising or falling?

21

A lot or a little? Before you decide that the weather is stable or changing, turn on the radio and listen, beyond the forecast. What are conditions five miles away? twenty miles away? How high are the seas in the channels and straits and in the open ocean? Spread out a chart that encompasses your entire cruising area—larger than that if you have one. Your anchorage is no bigger than the end of your thumb, your boat the point of a pencil. Imagine yourself flying high overhead, looking down. You may be in a pocket of calm while all around a gale is brewing. Or the wind that woke you may be entirely local, a dropping of cold air off a mountain, a funneling of air through a narrow entrance.

What do the trees on shore know? Are their boughs swaying? Or are the tops of the evergreens upright and still? If they are stunted and frozen, all the branches leaning inland, pay attention; they have been anchored here longer than you. Think of the weather that taught them to grow like that.

We shouldn't view the myriad things
from a human standpoint
because humans are integral
to the myriad things.

SHAKEDOWN

Clear of the harbor, we sail north under main and genoa. At last! Free from the city, free from our jobs. The past week has been a scramble, meeting deadlines at work and getting *Orca* ready after months at the dock. Was there anything that hadn't needed tuning or repairing or just plain cleaning?

My palms are black after coiling the halyards; probably should have cleaned the lines too. All that industrial grime is going with us, but I'm past caring. We're under way. During the next two weeks we won't so much as answer a telephone.

The sea is lively, as happy as we are to be in motion. Ten knots or so of wind, and the sails are full. Now and then a whitecap teases us along. The air is warm. Behind us the high-rise towers of Seattle recede. Hope I put enough stamps on that package—I didn't have time to wait in line at the post office today.

I go below to check on the stew. I have it figured so that dinner will be ready as soon as we anchor. The stew is simmering quietly in the big cast-iron pot on the stove. Everything's on schedule. Heading up the hatch with a couple of glasses of wine, I hear the hum of the propeller freewheeling, the tone slightly higher than usual under sail. I glance at the ship's clock: with the current and wind with us, as we'd planned, we're making great time. At this rate we'll be in Port Ludlow by sunset.

"Can you believe it's only five o'clock?" I say to Paul as we touch glasses in celebration of our escape. The freeways are clogged with commuters, and here we are, already on our way.

"I need to make a call when we get in," Paul replies. "I forgot to tell the engineer where that schematic is."

For the next two hours we seemed to fly, even-keeled under a clear sky. We didn't adjust the sails; we hardly touched the wheel. Everything had been hurry hurry, do this, do that, right up to casting off. What we hadn't finished—stowing gear on deck and clutter below—we could do tonight at anchor. We'd be ready when we crossed the Strait of Juan de Fuca tomorrow. For now we were happy to let *Orca* sail herself.

When we altered course slightly west toward Foul-weather Bluff, neither of us had the energy to take off the mizzen sail cover and run the lines. We'd be in port soon anyway. Instead, we sheeted in the main and genoa, then sheeted in further when we cleared the bluff, ready for a flawless reach to the entrance of Port Ludlow. Beyond, the sun was low, about to drop behind the jagged rim of the Olympic Mountains, pausing, it seemed, to guide us in. We would sleep well tonight.

It all happened in an instant. The wind hit the sails broadside. The toe rail dipped under, and everything on deck that wasn't tied down slid to starboard. From below came crashes, clunks, and one loud clang.

In the next instant the wind spilled from the downed sails and *Orca* righted herself, water streaming off her decks.

Our mouths made identical O's, and our eyes were wide. I scrambled to let out the main as Paul let out the genoa and eased the wheel to starboard. Completely awake now to where we were—not leaving, not arriving—we were sailing.

"What *happened*?" I started to ask, but the answer was obvious. Clear of the lee of Foulweather Bluff, we'd been suddenly exposed to the full length of Hood Canal. The brief blast that ambushed us was the same wind we'd coasted north on, intensified, something we should have been ready for. How could we have been so distracted?

We got in somewhat later than we'd expected, what with retrieving the oar that had gone over the side, and, fittingly enough, the overboard pole we hadn't secured. And what with stew all over the galley floor, it was past midnight when we got to bed.

Life is constantly changing
and our frame of mind
should change with it.

SMALL STUFF

Sunday mornings in the marina we always got together for breakfast. One week it would be on *Orca*, the next on *Godspeed*. Paul and I hadn't yet left for Alaska, but John and Bonni had already cruised there a couple times and made one crossing to Hawaii.

I liked sitting aboard *Godspeed*, sipping from a cup of steaming coffee. Though only 35 feet long, the ketch-rigged sailboat felt tidy and seaworthy. Everything had its place, and many things had multiple uses. The upholstered seats that ran fore and aft could be pulled out to make double beds in port or left narrow and enclosed with a lee cloth to make comfortable sea berths. The front-loading refrigerator in the galley could be used as a top-loading icebox accessible from the cockpit. They'd dispensed with the table, which, they complained, was useless under way and took up too much room, replacing it with a folding card table that could be stowed in a slot next to the companion-way ladder.

"What was it like in here on your way to Hawaii?" I asked one morning. We were still fitting out *Orca*'s interior, spending more time building than sailing. So far we'd made her comfortable for cruising between Seattle and Desolation Sound, but there were two ocean entrances on the Inside Passage to Alaska that we wanted to be ready for.

"Lumpy," Bonni said. I couldn't tell if her smile was

grim or amused. "We left San Diego in December and beat to weather all the way."

John nodded. "It was supposed to be a seventeen-day reach, nice and easy. Took us twenty-eight. Beautiful wind, but against us. At least we had the dodger by then, and the weather cloths. We would have been even wetter without them."

Dodger. Weather cloths. We'd need those to keep spray out of the hatch, out of the cockpit, and ultimately out of the cabin. We could use more handholds too; *Godspeed* had one every three or four feet.

"Remember how the portholes leaked?" Bonni put in. "There was so much pressure against them for so long, water was streaming through the gaskets." Renew porthole gaskets, I thought, goop them up with caulking and dog them down for the voyage. "We had to set a timer to remind us to wring out the towels every ten minutes. It's a good thing we had as many as we did— all those little hand towels we'd been given as wedding presents that we never thought we'd use."

A timer? Hand towels?

Bonni's face was animated and her eyes bright, though what she was describing sounded like work.

"And then there was the noise. With all that pounding, we about went nutty with the racket in here. It was impossible to sleep." She swept her arm around the cabin, and I imagined the sound of every object on every shelf and in every locker shifting, cans rattling against one another in the bilge, cutlery rattling in the drawers. Coastal cruising on *Orca,* we'd never had to put up with noise like that for long.

John smiled impishly, as if the entire experience had

been a joke played on them by the ocean that now gave him pleasure in the telling. "And just when we started to get used to it," he said, "we'd tack and everything would shift the other way. You can't have too many tiedowns." He plucked at a bungee cord, and Paul and I nodded; we'd learned that decorative fiddle rails weren't always high or strong enough to keep things from flying around. "Or"—he winked at Bonni—"ballpoint pens." And at that the two of them burst out laughing.

Paul and I looked blankly at each other.

"By the second week," John explained, "we'd managed to dampen most of the noise. But what kept driving us crazy were all these sliding panels." He tapped his hand against the small teak door behind him. Thunk-thunk. Thunk-thunk. Two closed in a bookshelf, and behind me were four that closed in cubbies. Looking around, I noticed similar doors in the galley and in the forward cabin, and I remembered others in the head. In order to slide smoothly, wood against wood, each small panel had to rest loosely in its grooves. Thunk-thunk. Off-watch, trying to sleep right here, *Godspeed* charging along—thunk-thunk. It could certainly get on your nerves.

"What saved our sanity was these." He picked up a ballpoint pen from the chart table, unscrewed it, and popped out the clicker. He handed the tiny cylinder of plastic to Paul.

Paul held it for a moment between his thumb and forefinger. "Very nice," he murmured. And before I'd caught on—I'd spent so many years writing with pens that I'd just assumed that the useful end was the point with the ink—he'd placed it upright in the space between panel and groove. The little cylinder fit perfectly. It rolled like a ball bearing as the panel slid open or shut. It silenced the rattle completely.

Everything has its own use,
regardless of some things'
seeming insignificance.

TO SAIL OR MOTOR?

The barometer hasn't budged, and the sky has a dreamy look, as if the weather itself had decided to nap for the rest of the day, too lazy to make a change. I move forward to take off the sail covers but stop myself. There's not that much wind. In every direction the water is calm. We'll barely move if we turn off the engine.

I look up at the masts and the rigging. What are they for if not to sail? A purist would definitely sail. But it's already midafternoon, and we're three hours from the anchorage if we keep motoring, more than double that if we sail. I can feel the engine, warm from running this past hour, rumble reassuringly beneath my feet.

Well, drifting a while could be pleasant. Drifting backward, that is; we'll be fighting the ebb. Making progress in light air against the current could turn out to be more frustrating than trying to make up my mind about sailing in the first place.

For a full ten minutes I argue with myself. Sail or keep motoring? Part of me wants to raise those sails and coax forward motion from this scant wind. I want to feel the gentle pull of white wings above us, the swaying motion the engine somehow dampens. But I want to get somewhere too, see the shoreline pass by at a steady rate. I'm looking forward to a do-nothing evening on the hook.

Paul's below making sandwiches, probably having this same discussion with the bread and cheese. When he comes on deck we'll talk, and unless I'm sure in my own mind, and he in his, we'll go round and round in a tiresome way that will ruin, really, the whole point of being out here. We're supposed to be getting away from petty concerns, not creating new ones.

A powerboat passes by to port. The people look carefree, undisturbed, so I imagine, by the question of propulsion. The long, smooth roll of their wake parallels our own, then curls slowly, and I dodge with the autopilot to meet it at an angle. *Orca*'s bow rises, falls, rises again, parting the wake with a splash that sounds like distant laughter. The autopilot swings us back on course toward Point Robinson, far to the south. Boats are clustered in the sunlight there, and when I pick up the binoculars, I see fishing poles and the sputter of trolling outboards. There are V shapes fluttering in the air and on the water, gulls calling in high-pitched, sobbing cries I cannot yet hear.

I turn the binoculars to starboard and pick out the

homes on Vashon Island, then scan for the telltale white head of an eagle amid the firs. I relax into a rhythm that asks nothing more of me today than my quiet attention.

Paul hands me a sandwich, and as I take it I know we'll keep motoring. I'm already doing what I want, and the absent, happy look on Paul's face tells me that he is too. No need to discuss anything. Smiling, we settle into the cockpit, and the engine purrs on.

If your mind is torn by
two conflicting desires,
the contradiction will destroy
your mind's unity and
tranquility.

PROVISIONING

I took to provisioning with gusto. Everything about stocking up on necessary supplies for the galley energized me: figuring out what we'd eat, imagining each breakfast, each dinner. It was like I was already cruising. No matter how long the voyage—two days, two weeks—I inventoried, made a list, planned ahead.

So when it came time to provision for our six-week cruise up the Inside Passage to Alaska, I was ready for the challenge.

As I traced the trip on charts, it became clear that for much of the voyage we'd be in wilderness. We couldn't count on resupplying along the way. Best to follow the example of ocean sailors, whose articles I'd been reading in boating magazines. They described at length what to buy, how to label and date the tops of cans with grease pencil, how to rotate eggs so they'd last. Invariably they were photographed cross-legged on the dock among boxes and boxes of food, impressive proof that they were smart, frugal, and prepared.

Dutifully, I made a list. Since the boat's refrigerator at the time was an old battery-guzzler and we wanted to sail as often as we could, my list consisted mostly of canned goods in quantities that seemed prudent at the time. Pounds of rice, flour, pasta, dried beans, potatoes, and onions. Many dozens of eggs. Three bottles of catsup. Six cans of pickled beets. Eight cans of artichoke hearts. Twelve cans each of green beans, mushroom soup, tomato soup. Twenty-four cans of whole tomatoes and as many cans of tomato paste. And then there were toiletries: six tubes of toothpaste, twenty rolls each of toilet paper and paper towels.

The list was six pages long.

It took a day in a borrowed pickup to buy all the provisions. When we loaded them in the boat, the boxes and sacks covered every horizontal surface; we were too tired to take a picture. It took two days to stow everything. That was a job in itself, finding places for it all. Canned goods went on top of the fuel tank. Eggs in the bilge. Flour under the berth. Toilet paper everywhere.

I was pretty proud of myself afterward, but of course I then had to make another list to remind me where everything was. Admittedly, the waterline lowered with the added weight, but I figured that since we'd be eating as we went along, any sluggishness in the boat's performance would be short-lived.

The Inside Passage to Alaska isn't open ocean, but we went many days without seeing a village or town once we got past the rapids above Desolation Sound. The land was raw and green, and the forests grew right down to the water. The most we saw for days was a cluster of cabins around an abandoned cannery. But the fish—cod, salmon, halibut—were easy to catch, and crab too. Neither of us wanted to eat canned soup, chili, or corned beef. It was late summer, the blueberries were fat on the bushes, and the fruit cocktail we'd stowed was spectacularly unappealing. Of course we'd dip into our supplies, but not deeply, and though we ate simply, even monotonously, by any standard we ate well.

On our way to Bishop Hot Springs we met a man in a small boat who needed a tow to Hartley Bay for gas. It was hours out of our way, but we weren't on a schedule and the detour gave us an excuse to backtrack through the fjord around Gribbell Island, which we were told was drop-dead gorgeous. As for Hartley Bay itself, the only description we could find was of an Indian village with a "seasonal fuel dock and limited food supplies."

On the outside chance that it would have fresh produce—one of the few things we craved by now—I went looking for the store when we arrived. The store was up the hill on a dirt road in what seemed from the outside to be a private home. I knocked on the front door—it didn't feel right to just walk in—and a soft-voiced woman invited me in through her living room to the kitchen. The barge that delivered their weekly produce had been in two days ago, she apologized, and all that was left for sale was some limp lettuce. But what she had was even better: a freezer case filled with five-gallon tubs of hard ice cream. While she filled two cones with generous scoops of chocolate and strawberry, I perused the rest of the shelves. They were stocked—well stocked—with canned goods, rice, flour, sugar, and pasta. Almost exactly what I'd thought would be impossible to find. And toilet paper. Plenty of toilet paper. How could I have thought there wouldn't be?

At least the prices were high.

Even this point was eventually lost. During the four years we lived in Alaska, and later, long after we'd cruised back to Seattle, I'd periodically pull a can from the top of the fuel tank that was swollen from spoilage or so old that it wasn't worth the risk of opening. Even later, ten years after my grand provisioning, I ran across two forgotten plastic buckets in the very aft corner of a locker behind the companionway ladder. I hauled them out by their handles and with some effort pried off the lids. Inside were bags of sugar, boxes of cake mix, and a ten-pound bag of flour the size of a concrete block and just as hard. I thought wryly of the money spent to buy those sacks, the time spent carrying them from the store to the car to the dock and into the locker where they had rested all those years, nourishing nothing but the tiny bugs that now swarmed inside them.

Hadn't I been economical and efficient?

Everything reverses direction

upon reaching its extreme.

WEATHERED IN

There was no way we were going to cross Queen Charlotte Sound that day, much as we wanted to. Gale warnings, winds to forty knots, seas to fifteen feet. We'd stay where we were and wait it out.

Something about the word *wait* makes me fret. Instead of relaxing in the present, I lean into the future. Being where I am seems enforced, and I look for ways to break free.

Short of stupidly throwing ourselves into a rough sea, there was no freedom from this little inlet. We'd anchored up one of the protective narrow arms, but what had seemed so welcoming when we thought we would be there only one night now seemed to wall us in. Huge cedar and fir grew thick, straight up from the steep shore. No relief of beach, let alone a suggestion anywhere of a trail. We were stuck on the water.

Not that going ashore had much appeal when the rain started. An artist wouldn't need a colored palette in this climate, I thought, looking out the pilothouse windows. Rain streaked the view, which was every shade of gray: ashy boughs against striated trunks the color of wet cement, a low, pewter sky. Dull and spirit-flattening. I felt submerged in the grayness, my movements slowed, my vision dimmed. The water itself wasn't gray, though; it was tea-colored.

Paul was napping in the main cabin, a book spread open on his chest. I reached for my own book and wandered into another time and place until, hours later, my shoulders and back demanded activity.

I stood and stretched. Wisps of rust-colored foam on the rain-pocked water moved steadily out the inlet. Must be a stream somewhere back up there.

"Did you say something?" Paul asked. He was now taking apart a fishing reel on the galley table, trying to figure out why it wouldn't cast.

"This foam," I said, "I wonder where it comes from."

"The rain's let up some. Wanna find out?"

We pulled on our rain gear—boots, bib pants, the works—and launched the dinghy. We both wanted the exercise, so we took turns rowing. The farther up the inlet we rowed, the stronger the current was against us, and the more foam there was on the brown water. I dipped my finger and licked; it was only faintly salty.

We heard rushing water, and turning a corner, we saw the rocks, the spilling lagoon beyond, and everywhere billowing, swirling foam, enormous suds in a giant bubble bath.

We looked at each other, eyes shining, and Paul rowed right in. He shipped the oars, and the current carried us, laughing, the foam circling us like sheep, crowding over the gunwale and filling the dinghy with bubbles that hissed and disappeared. Back in again, and again, and out with the current, whirling in the rain.

Seize the moment;
experience the present;
don't let anything slip by.

HAULED OUT

As those of us with boats know, the worst part of yearly maintenance is hauling out. Not because the work itself is difficult but because the entire process is so profoundly disorienting. In order to scrub the bottom free of barnacles and seaweed and brush on fresh antifouling paint, you have to take the boat out of the water, exactly where boats are not made to be. The boat is unresponsive, suspended, almost dead, like a body on anesthesia during surgery. A house shaking during an earthquake triggers the same message: *something's terribly wrong.*

Boatyards in the Lower 48 have hoists and marine

ways that mechanically lift the hull out of the water, but in Juneau large boats have to haul out on "the grid." At high tide the grid looks like nothing more than a long, extra-stout pier. Every ten feet or so is a spigot, a power outlet, and a ladder that drops straight down into the water. For an incredibly small fee—twenty dollars a day when we lived there—a skipper can tie to these timbers at high tide. And wait. And fret. For as the tide recedes, lines must be adjusted, the boat kept parallel and close to the pilings. Eventually the boat, dropping with the level of the water, settles down on a shelf of timbers. When the water drops below the timbers and the boat's entire belly is exposed, the scraping, scrubbing, drying down, and painting begins. The pace is steadily frantic; in less than six hours the water will be lapping at the soles of your rubber boots. Then your ankles, then your shins. And then you've run out of time.

Our first experience with the Juneau grid was a bad one. We had arrived only a day or two before, and oblivious to the heavy dark clouds, not even checking the forecast—*hey, it was August*—we motored over to the grid at high tide.

Our cockiness was exposed right away. We were still positioning *Orca* when the tide turned; too late, we realized we were stuck, three feet away from the pilings. *Orca* settled astern first, and in a breathless moment we tossed a line to a man standing on the pier, who pulled the bow parallel. A minute later we were aground on the timbers. Inch by inch—I could see it plainly—the water dropped away. In less than twenty minutes *Orca* was left standing tiptoe on her keel. If she fell either way, she would be gravely damaged.

I felt sick. Never before had *Orca* been so vulnerable. How could we have done this? *Orca* wasn't a toy; she was our home, and everything we owned—tools, clothes, dishes and pots, photos and books, lamps, rugs, bedding—was aboard. Everything.

But there was no time for blame or regret. We had to secure her as best we could, right now. Moving slowly so as not to disturb her balance, Paul and I positioned a plank between *Orca*'s rail and the pier. We added a web of lines between her and the pilings, then ran the main and mizzen halyards from the top of the masts to other pilings on shore—desperate attempts to give her some type of support. We carefully hauled the anchor chain amidships, hoping the weight would do more good there. We barely talked.

As though holding her breath, *Orca* did not move. There was no wind. I cannot remember any sound. A small group of fishermen gathered and dispersed, then another. It began to rain. Not drops but streams of rain. We stood in the muck as though in a waterfall, looking up at our boat.

Better to stay off of her, and since we had the time and adrenaline, better to scrub her down than do nothing at all. Under our stiff brushes and the spray of water from our hose, not to mention the slick of rain flowing down the hull, the red bottom paint sloughed away. It was wasted work, for the rain never let up long enough for us to repaint. About the only useful thing we did was change zincs; at least the propeller and through-hull fittings wouldn't corrode. It was getting dark now—almost ten o'clock—and we still had four more hours before the tide would begin to rise.

For four hours we watched *Orca* in the dark and the rain. Neither of us wanted to leave. It would have been like abandoning a friend who was in trouble because of us. I think we both believed that our fear and hope for *Orca* would keep her balanced there.

I swore that I would never go out on a grid again. But by the next spring *Orca*'s hull had a thick crust of barnacles. We approached that haulout with the care of soldiers going into battle. We studied the tide tables, looking for the weekend with the longest low tide and a backup weekend in case of bad rain. We assembled all the tools and supplies we would need, and extra besides. We asked for advice and help. We used more care.

It often happens that
our greatest troubles arise
from ourselves.

THE RIGHT BAIT

Fishing poles propped between our legs, Paul and I floated on the fringes of Icy Strait in our inflatable dinghy, hoping something would bite.

There was lots of biting going on. Gulls screamed and dove. Puffins and grebes surfaced, their bills full of wriggling silver. On the far side of the Strait, beneath the slate-gray sky, humpback whales snorted and blew.

We were dressed for Southeast Alaska's usual May weather: yellow rain gear over jeans, wool sweaters, and thermal underwear, the collars of our jackets turned up to touch our wool caps. I wore mittens; Paul, more resistant to cold, wore fingerless wool gloves.

Over and over we tried the technique that had yielded halibut in the past: motor to an area over a shelf where the bottom rises; kill the engine and toss the sea anchor over the side to help hold position; pay out fishing line until the lead weight hits the bottom. A few clicks back on the reel and wait.

Waiting, I imagine the fish I will catch. It is lying on its left side, both eyes up. Its mouth opens and closes silently, sensing the water for motion and food. Its gills rise and fall. With any luck, I have dropped my bait directly in front of this fish, where it floats sinuously.

"Nothing," Paul finally said. A simple statement, not a complaint. "We must have missed the tide."

"That, or we're too early in the season," I offered. "It's

been cold—maybe they're still deep." The thought made me reel in with finality; by now my toes were numb and my nose was dripping. My line, not to mention my patience in this gray cold, wasn't long enough to reach halibut in their winter holes. Paul followed my lead.

Of course, the problem of catching a fish remained, of returning empty-handed to Swanson Harbor. We were the only pleasure boat there. While we had been fishing so leisurely, for sport, commercial crews had been in a manic state of preparation for the halibut opening ahead. For the past two days they'd been making repairs, cutting bait, lining washtubs with sets of hooks and gangens. This opening would be a short one—only thirty-six hours to catch as many halibut as they could. There would be no sleep and little real eating; already, getting prepared, men were spooning cold soup from opened cans, pawing through boxes of stale donuts.

The fish were around, I thought to myself over the drone of the outboard as we wove through the rocks into Swanson Harbor. All those fishermen were counting on it. They would catch what we had not.

I rummaged through a locker in the galley, feeling for the familiar crackling of cellophane. On the back of the sack was the recipe: Toll House cookies. Measuring and mixing next to the stove warmed me through and through, and soon the boat was filled with the soft sweetness of nutmeg, brown sugar, and melting chocolate.

Outside, the pace was quickening. Engines were started, checked, restarted. Paul, up from his nap, was donating lengths of fuel hose and wire, the odd clamp or fastening—whatever he had among his tools that seemed to be needed. I carefully put the cookies into sacks; they breathed warmly through the brown paper, staining the sides and bottoms.

As the four boats cast off that evening I handed a sack to each skipper. Their puzzled, distracted faces lit up at the sight and smell of the contents. "Good luck," I said. "Here's something to get you through."

The next day Paul motored out alone to try again. I stayed behind to make cinnamon rolls.

Like baking the cookies, this was a fragrant job, but a little more complicated. During the ten minutes I kneaded the soft dough, I thought of the crews on Icy Strait, dropping their baited, barbed skates, then waiting for the right time to winch them back up. Then the huge flat fish, all enraged muscle, would be unhooked, subdued, slapped into the hold, and the next set made. All I had to do was wait an hour or so through the first rising, then pat out the dough, sprinkle it with sugar and raisins, roll, cut, and plop into baking pans. In order that the rolls would be fresh from the oven when the fishing boats returned, I merely timed the second rising to take place overnight in the cockpit, where temperatures would drop below forty degrees.

The growl of prop wash woke me the next morning. I turned up the diesel stove and slid in the baking pans, each crowded with swollen spirals of dough bursting with raisins and cinnamon. Thirty minutes later I pulled them out, golden and overwhelmingly fragrant. Paul, whose fishing efforts had been skunked the day before, painted the tops with icing and arranged them on four paper plates, stacking the rolls like children's blocks.

We put on our jackets and climbed out the hatch, plates in our hands. Outside, all was gray. On the aft deck of the nearest boat stood two men in yellow bib rain pants smeared with slime and blood. Dead halibut were layered around them almost to their shins. They held white-handled knives with thin, slightly curved blades. One held a halibut, big as a manhole cover, by its tail, white underbelly up on the cutting table, ready for gutting. Amid the slaughter, the men's faces were vacant and tired.

"Good morning," I said, offering up a plate of cinnamon rolls.

Instantly the exhaustion disappeared. Wiping their hands on their sleeves and grinning broadly, they took the plate and sat on the rail. "Grab that pot of coffee," one said as the other reached into the pilothouse for paper towels. "This is great!"

I smiled back and moved on to the next boat.

By noon the boats had motored off to sell their

catch. Four halibut, cleanly gutted, had been left on our deck.

There is not just one path,
and not everyone is fit
to travel the same path.

FOLLOWING SEAS

While we slept a gale was born in the Gulf of Alaska. It veered east toward Frederick Sound and was caught in the maze of the Southeast archipelago. Bounded by two- and three-thousand-foot mountains, it turned northward to scream up Stephens Passage right into our anchorage. We had no choice but to leave.

It was four o'clock in the morning and already full daylight. Getting under way was a blur; what I remembered most was the keening aloft, how the dark line on the water broadened in our direction, and most especially the icebergs, blue-white and as big as *Orca*, that advanced toward us on the wind.

I was disoriented from sleeplessness, the rush of raising anchor, and a touch of nausea. Paul looked better than I felt, but not much. I knew he was berating himself—as I was berating myself—for not listening to the forecast before we went to bed. We'd been seduced by the calm and by the champagne, which now tasted sour in my mouth.

No time for the luxury of regret. The nearest shelter was Taku Inlet, twenty miles to the north, a three-hour run under power in worsening weather and steepening seas. As we motored out of Holkham Bay neither of us brought up sailing, though the wind and seas would be with us once we headed north. Too tricky in these conditions—in *our* condition was more like it. Let's just get this over with.

When the weather is fair a following sea is a joy. A gale is another matter. The seas, piling up behind you, want to swing you around and roll you over in a broach. You try to stay on top of the swells, to go neither too fast nor too slow, and above all keep the boat from sliding sideways. It doesn't help that each wave lifting the stern potentially decreases the effectiveness of the rudder and every trough threatens to bury the bow.

I forced these dire consequences from my thoughts. Conditions weren't that dangerous, just profoundly uncomfortable, especially as I lurched through the cabin, latching down every drawer and door, putting everything on the table in the deep sink. Never again, I vowed, would I leave the galley in such a mess before turning in at anchor.

It was actually less chaotic in the cockpit, where

the rising gale had a rhythm I could see. Behind us the whitecaps crested and curled. The backs of the waves, streaked with white foam, rolled ahead of us. Twenty knots of wind? twenty-five? I watched Paul, trying to remember how to tend the helm in a following sea; sooner or later I'd be at the wheel. A wave would raise the stern, and just when it seemed that *Orca* was about to slide sideways he would straighten the bow and she would rise. Now and then a taller or steeper or maybe just faster wave would break the pattern and slam hard against the transom. For a sickening moment gravity would be suspended. I held on, Paul wrestled the wheel, and our whole world rocked and swayed and continued on. How had he done that?

"I need a break," Paul said when we passed Midway

Island. I nodded. My turn. And just as he had done in the past hour, I learned again what I already knew.

At first I oversteered, but even as the boat wallowed *Orca*'s broad beam and long, deep keel forgave me, and I was able to resume our course. I wasn't clutching the cockpit coaming or crouching in the hatch. I wasn't looking back at ever darker water and ever higher seas, trying to calculate the wind speed from the streaked, gray-green surface. I was standing, centered, looking ahead, feeling the sea and the hull through my flexed legs, the position of the rudder through my arms. The lift of the stern signaled each wave, and I turned the wheel to take it on the aft quarter. When I got it right, the wave itself seemed to straighten us, so that *Orca* was eased, not pushed, in the direction I wanted to go. I was neither in control nor out of control. *Orca* heaved up, stern, then bow, rolling gently, and the sea hissed as it carried us along.

What other people have come
to understand intuitively
can never become yours
unless you come to understand it
through your own efforts.

THE BROKEN IMPELLER

We were furling the sails when the high-pitched alarm sounded. Paul disappeared below, and seconds later the engine stopped.

"Water temperature," he called from the hatch. "We swallowed an impeller blade."

I continued tying sail stops along the main boom, unconcerned. We always carried a spare impeller; anything could be sucked up the water intake and foul those little rubber blades. Meanwhile, we had plenty of sea room here in the middle of Taku Inlet. Not much time though. We'd lowered the sails just now in order to make Taku Harbor—our favorite weekend getaway—before night fell. Summer was short in Southeast Alaska. Already, in early September, darkness was advancing, minutes per day, on what only a month ago had seemed like endless daylight. In this overcast the night would blacken everything completely.

"Honey?" It was Paul again. "Do you know where I put those spares?" At the sight of my face—I clearly didn't—Paul's tightened. Without an impeller to pump cooling water to the diesel it would overheat. Within minutes we'd be dead in the water with a damaged engine.

"Better get these sails back up," I said, trying not to sound disappointed. We'd have to go back to Juneau, of course. We couldn't stay where we were, drifting, or grope our way blindly along an unmarked shore under sail. "At least the wind's going our way," I sighed.

"It's rising a bit too!" Paul joined me on the foredeck,

all the tension in his face replaced by the prospect of action. "We should be able to sail right up the channel, then turn on the engine when we get near the city dock— just for a few minutes." He made it sound so simple.

We raised sail in the falling light. Handling lines and cranking winches soon displaced my regret over abandoning the getaway we'd been looking forward to. We let the main out to port, the working jib to starboard, wing and wing. The wind blew steadily, and with only a few adjustments the two sails balanced each other.

In the first half-hour we were busy and talkative, taking compass bearings on landmarks while they were still visible, taking turns eating dinner below, putting on extra clothing against the chill. With the darkness we fell silent and watchful.

I had never sailed through such blackness, and at first it disoriented and mesmerized me. Not a boat on the water anywhere, not a cabin on land; for that matter, no distinction between water and land. We were a moving island, a capsule in space. The masthead light was the only star in the black sky. The running lights glowed red on the port deck, green on the starboard, and their color spilled over the rail and onto the ink of the sea. The stern light turned our wake to molten silver. Around us the phosphorescent whitecaps renewed themselves tirelessly on the wind. And the luminous white sails never faltered.

Every six seconds the light on tiny Marmion Island flashed. When we passed it, entering the narrow fjord of Gastineau Channel, I felt more than saw the mountains that rose above us, thousands of feet straight up; patches of snow that had survived the summer delineated the highest peaks. In the darkness they seemed magnified. Ahead, Juneau was a dimness that slowly brightened at the foot of Mount Roberts. As we approached, propelled by the following wind and current, houses took shape, then roads and cars and office buildings.

It did not seem like the familiar city where we lived and worked, the city we had left only five hours ago, but a newly discovered place, the end of a wonderful voyage, a refuge we had earned.

*We often discover a certain joy in
hardship after the hardship is over.
If we can discover it
while it is happening,
then winter will have its wonders.*

ON THE HOOK

You've found a cove that will protect you from wind and wave. You've dropped the anchor and let out plenty of chain and then backed down to set the flukes deep into the mud. You've checked the tide tables to make sure you have enough scope so that even if the wind were to find you, the anchor would hold. You've taken bearings against the shore and determined that, no, you're not drifting, just swinging and recoiling a bit. And the engine finally is silent.

I love those first moments, when the silence is like a sound in itself. Suddenly I realize that all I've really been listening to under way was the boat's rumbling engine, thrumming sails, and turning propeller. The boat still speaks—every now and then the anchor chain moves against the bobstay with a dull clunk, or a loose halyard slaps the mast—but now my ears are tuned beyond the gunwale and the bowsprit, higher than the masthead. Birds cry, or caw, or whistle musical scales across the water. Wavelets whisper to the beach.

No longer checking the instruments or reading a chart, watching the leech of the sail or the telltales near the luff, I notice other details. Shadows of the evergreens move over the rocks, down the beach, and reach for us across the water. A rippled circle spreads outward where a grebe just dove, or a fish just leapt, or a seal slipped, nose last, beneath the surface. A tree branch sags where a large bird—an eagle? a raven?—has just perched.

No longer navigating the boat, I watch the course of objects in the sky. The sun tracks westward, gathering gold as it drops. When it sets, color goes with it, until what was fuchsia is pink and what was pink is violet, then gray, then black. The stars that had been there all along come forward quietly until the sky is a riot of light. When the moon rises, it dims the stars.

I will sleep lightly at anchor, for the boat is still moving, gently swaying, slowly swinging with the current. It rocks freely to a passing wake, unrestrained by dock lines and fenders. It revolves like a planet around the fixed pole of the anchor. There's the sea, below and around, and the sky and the land which seem to grow from the sea. There's the boat suspended between, and me in the boat, dreaming shallow dreams, still listening.

And when the anchor is raised and the boat is under way once more, for a moment I'll feel that a part of me was left behind and is rushing to catch up.

We should become one
with our surroundings,
forget ourselves in the world around us,
and enter the one single
raindrop between heaven and earth.

AGAINST THE SEA

The whole wide Gulf of Alaska seemed to be crashing against the entrance to Lisianski Strait. We'd been motoring since dawn from Elfin Cove, on the inside of Yakobi Island, in order to give the seas from last night's gale a chance to quiet down. For the past three hours we'd been in water so still the steep shore reflected perfectly, upside down. Now *Orca* was responding to swells that rolled up the narrow entrance. I could see the high black rocks in silhouette against the gray horizon; with each wave, the sea covered them with froth.

I bit my lip. So far I'd been able to channel my anxiety into preparation. Everything below and on deck was secure. I'd made sandwiches and a thermos of soup so I could stay out of the galley if it got too rough. I had on my full rain gear. But I couldn't erase the deep vertical line of worry between my eyebrows.

Paul, in annoying contrast, was bright-eyed and smiling, as if he relished what was ahead. He'd been checking the engine and the water, fuel, and oil levels, tightening hose clamps, writing in the log. He'd rigged the working jib, the foresail, and the main—already reefed—so they could be raised as soon as we cleared the rocks. And what rocks! Where we were headed, the chart was all crosses and asterisks, a galaxy of rocks exposed, submerged, and awash. It could be a wild ride steering clear of those rocks under power, then staying far enough offshore under sail.

I ticked off the reasons we had chosen this route. The weather was gradually improving over the outside waters, degrading rapidly inside, and the barometer was rising—the surest sign of fair skies and winds. Going outside Chichagof Island was shorter than weaving our way to Sitka through Peril Strait. And just as important, we'd never been this way before.

So I girded myself mentally for the impending struggle with the elements. If green water broke over the deck, I was rubberized to meet it. A sudden lurch? I was harnessed up. Seasick? I had home remedies in the cockpit—raisins, celery and carrot sticks, soda crackers, candied ginger. Bottled water and ginger ale. Macho woman! I was fully armed.

If only I could look and feel like I was enjoying this. The first big swell was almost a relief. *Orca* lifted, then dropped into the trough, cleaving the green water so that it flared away from her bow. More swells, and then they were coming from two directions at once as the ocean, battering through the entrance, spent its anger on the rocks.

"We should be out of this in fifteen minutes," Paul said when he saw my grim face. "Thirty at most." His hands were busy at the wheel but did not, I noticed, have the death grip mine did on the cockpit cleat.

I set my teeth and nodded. *Orca* was pounding a bit but still making way; as usual, she and Paul were taking conditions in stride. I hunkered down inside myself as if enduring a kind of punishment. Maybe this hammering was payment for the spectacular days we'd just had in Glacier Bay.

I kept my eyes ahead, beyond the rocks. I didn't

want to look to the side, where kelp heaved on the seas. But something moved on the periphery of my gaze in a way that caused me to turn my head and look.

It was an otter. Not a sleek river otter, but a round-headed, fuzzy sea otter, floating half-submerged in the furious water near a pinnacle rock. The otter lounged on its back, front paws resting on its chest, hind paws spread nonchalantly beyond its belly, and it turned its head to watch us for a moment, like an old man on a porch swing who sees a car he doesn't know passing through his neighborhood and wonders who it is, and what's the rush.

"Nice day!" I half expected the otter to shout, and for a moment it seemed about to wave but scratched its chin instead.

I waved back anyway and in that gesture tossed all the tension I was feeling over the side. For when I faced the ocean again I was rising and falling with *Orca* like the otter and the kelp, moving easily with the sea.

The way of nature is to win

without contending.

SAILS, ENGINES, OARS, AND PADDLES

We pulled *Orca* into our new marina on a brilliant August afternoon. It had been a long voyage—over a month on the inside and outside waters between Glacier Bay and Seattle. So many new harbors and ports, so much change and motion; the boats in the marina looked as if they'd never moved, and never would.

A man stepped onto the dock from a powerboat moored near the slip we were heading for. "Can I take your line?" he asked, tossing his cigarette into the water. He was lean, neither young nor old, with a weathered face that was all angles and squints. Something about the way he stood and handled the line I tossed him made me think he was more cowboy than mariner.

His boat was forty-five feet long with a fiberglass hull and spare decks. The cabin and pilothouse were roomy and tall, and so clean. *Orca*'s house was low, and the deck was cluttered with cruising gear: boat poles, crab pots, buckets, a salmon net and fishing poles, to say nothing of the winches, fairleads, cleats, and belaying pins needed for sailing. Almost the same length overall, but with a lot less living space inside. Paul and I had never considered a powerboat. Sailing was the way to get where we wanted to go eventually—New Zealand—and the way to cruise in the meantime, between Puget Sound and Alaska.

A boat for inland waters, I concluded of our new neighbor's powerboat. Folding chairs on the aft deck, a table with an umbrella, only one anchor. And look at all those windows! Dangerous, I imagined, in a rough sea.

The letters on the stern read *Baralku*, a bit too fancy considering the boat's unassuming appearance and the no-nonsense manner of its owner, Al. But I supposed there was a story behind the name, possibly a dream, and one afternoon I asked. Moored so close, working on our boats side by side, we'd often fall into aimless cross-dock conversation.

"Where does the name *Baralku* come from?"

"It's a mythical island. Aboriginal Australian."

I straightened up from my work sanding the cabin. Australia. I envisioned that strange continent, a dateline and a huge ocean away to the west. Farther away, even, than New Zealand. "Have you been there?" I asked, expecting to hear about a vacation he and his wife had taken since he retired.

"Couple years ago. Helen and I had a great time. Favorite anchorage was near Cairns."

Anchorage? "You went there in your *boat*?"

"Yeah." He laughed, and rested his forearms on *Baralku*'s waist-high rail. The chisel he'd been using to chase rot in the toerail dangled from his hands. "That's what everyone said over there, too. One sailboater insisted it was impossible." He shrugged, as he had probably shrugged then, unconcerned about anyone else's disbelief. He'd done it; there was nothing special really—just find the calms and head right into them. "What you sailors don't do," he grinned, tapping a Pall Mall from a pack and lighting it.

I looked at *Baralku* as if for the first time. The flared bow. The heavy stockless anchor, like the ones commercial fishing boats use. The stabilizing poles I'd assumed were for show. Below were fuel tanks, not a spacious salon, and a serious diesel—two in-line, as it turned out, one a backup that he hadn't needed so far.

In Alaska we'd met people who'd rowed or kayaked the entire Inside Passage, which was remarkable enough, and humbling too. Here in Seattle was someone who'd "driven" to Australia.

The next year Al drove to Hawaii and back, alone, with no fanfare that Paul or I could see. A few years later he and his wife drove to New Zealand. And all the while we stayed behind at our jobs, sailing on weekends in our own oceangoing vessel.

By emphasizing appearances,
   we miss the real thing.

FOGBOUND

Fogbound. Water and air have fused, and the whole world is white, without horizon. Air is water, water is air, the land is swallowed, gone. The sun is a white disk you can look at with eyes wide open, as if it were the moon. You're wrapped in chill, moist gauze, no clear vision beyond your bow, at times not even as far as your bow.

Straight up the sky is almost blue. You long to climb to the top of the mast, to see clearly again, but even this wouldn't work; all would be gray-white froth below. Thickening, the fog obscures the sun completely.

You listen for the fog signal coming from land, two

low moans every thirty seconds. "HORN (2) 30s," it says on the chart; ahead is Point No Point, but how far ahead? You jot down the time. Another horn sounds, a long blast—somewhere a ship. You answer with your own, remembering the rules for running blind: one long blast every two minutes.

Thank god for instruments. Radar with its blips, all the three-dimensional world reduced to a monochrome screen you make yourself trust. There are others out there, groping as you are. What does your boat look like on their screens? Some don't have radar. Some don't even have radar reflectors: fishing skiffs, runabouts, kayaks. One could appear in front of you now. You strain to see ahead. A shadow becomes a boat, sailing in the opposite direction, and you all wave like idiots, as if five hundred feet of visibility were some sort of triumph.

The depth-sounder flashes as you follow a ten-fathom line to stay out of the shipping lanes. What on earth are you doing out here? It didn't look so bad when you weighed anchor, but now you're wondering why you didn't stay put. Motoring dead slow, timing signals, remembering to sound your own—this fog is as exhausting as a gale, all your senses tuned so high for so long. The fog fills your vision with mist, distorts sound so that your eyes strain as you listen.

No wonder, in the golden days of sail, sailors spent most of their time in port or at anchor, waiting.

Something tall and dark emerges, and you brace yourself instinctively for a freighter bearing down, sounding the signal for danger. But it's only a sandy bluff with an evergreen top, disguised by the shifting fog and your imagination. A headland—you can see it on the radar, a little too close, perhaps; the current has pushed you a bit. You turn the wheel to correct your course, when dead ahead you see splashes. *Rocks! Impossible!* Heart pounding, you go into full reverse, fumble for the chart. *Where are we?* All of your judgment and all your instruments are suddenly and completely in doubt.

Then one of the rocks flashes a flipper, a fluke—*porpoise.* You laugh with relief and joy as they play beneath your bow.

Fog doesn't lift. It dissolves. And before your eyes are bright blue channels, green islands, brown beaches, black rocks, white boats. The world is given back to you, and for a while it seems newly made. Behind, the retreating fog is a blur of white and gray. It wraps around an island, hides it completely, reveals it, hides it again. It lets you go.

If we can overcome the
inherent limitations of our senses,
using our eyes to hear,
and our ears to see,
suddenly everything will
become clear.

CONVENIENCES, COMFORTS, AND UPGRADES

It begins as a convenience.

Wouldn't refrigeration be great? No more buying ice and hauling it down the dock. You could freeze those fish when you caught 'em. You could eat ice cream afloat.

So you shop around for a refrigeration system that will fit. You add more insulation to the box. You clear a space in the engine room or lazarette that's big enough for the compressor and drill the holes to mount it. Then you drill more holes for the copper tubing that runs between it and the evaporator. The whole system needs power, so you add a breaker to the circuit panel and run wire through lockers and the overhead. You do all this on your back, on your stomach, on your knees, more often than not with your rear in the air. You turn the refrigerator on, the frost forms a satisfying fuzz inside the little freezer compartment, and it's all worth it. The milk stays cold. The lettuce stays crisp.

But.

The refrigerator devours batteries. At anchor or under sail you have to run the engine for an hour a day to keep the batteries up. The ice cream still goes soft. You install a new alternator with more output. You add another battery. Now you need another system to monitor the batteries. Meanwhile, the chilled copper tubing sweats in the warm locker, drips on the plywood, and starts the silent cancer of dry rot.

Or it begins as a creature comfort.

Wouldn't it be nice to have a bigger settee? You could stretch out after a day of cruising, relax, and read. There would be more seating around the table too.

So you tear out the old settee. It isn't easy. Everything's glued and screwed and built to stay. The flooring gets a little chewed up, but that needs refinishing anyway. You never liked those shelves against the hull—too short for books. Now's as good a time as any to rebuild them. If you lengthen the settee just a little, it could work as another berth in here. This requires making an existing locker six inches narrower. The table you carefully removed and planned to reinstall is now too small for the U shape of the enlarged settee. Looking for upholstery that matches, you fall in love with a soft blue leather and order new cushions all around. As the new settee takes shape you wonder why you didn't do this long ago.

Then.

The rest of the interior looks shabby. There's sawdust everywhere. Might as well refinish all the teak and repaint all the bulkheads. Maybe try a new wallcovering. And what about the galley? It could use a new countertop.

Often it begins with the simple desire for something new.

That old depth-sounder—a flasher from the seventies—isn't it time to upgrade? Sure, it works, but it takes up a lot of room. The new ones are smaller, and do more.

You spend hours researching what the dealers call your "options." A unit the same size as the one you have is not only a depth-sounder but also a radar. The new unit has a GPS, charts for the entire world that you can bring up on the screen, and tide and current tables.

However.

The new depth-sounder uses a transducer that's different from the one you already have. When you haul the boat out to put it in, you end up spending an entire morning removing the old one. Snaking the cable up to the depth-sounder, you realize that the holes are too small. Enlarging them, you pray you don't drill through the other wires. You drill more holes and pull more cable installing the new radar antenna. The new depth-sounder itself is slightly smaller than the old one. The existing hole looks ragged—better replace the entire instrument panel. Maybe it's time for new gauges and switches, go for one of those vessel management systems. Put in a new radio, a cell phone, a weather station. Upgrade the autopilot so it'll link to the new electronics. You imagine yourself at the helm with all new controls, like a pilot in a jet airplane. You know you're going to want another one of everything for the flying bridge.

And all the while, your boat is at the dock or in the yard, engine silent, sails stowed.

Don't pursue a superfluous amount
of material things, otherwise
you will become a slave to them.

SHORTENING SAIL

We left Friday Harbor at the tail end of the ebb. Blue sky, puffy white clouds, ten to fifteen knots of wind from the south—we had the sails up and set by the time we'd motored into San Juan Channel. From bowsprit to pilot-house the genoa stood, cupped and full and perfect as a shell. The main and mizzen curved to embrace the moving air. Heeling gracefully, *Orca* tracked the seas as surely as a plow, a white foamy wake peeling from her bow.

The wind was on our nose, but the current was still with us, and we didn't have far to go—less than ten miles to Mackaye Harbor. We could easily sail all the way. We were homeward now after weeks of sailing, motoring, and anchoring, and *Orca* was no longer a piece of machinery we maneuvered, fumbling at times, overcorrecting at others. Our interaction with *Orca* was more like a conversation, the listening as important as the talking.

Not half an hour out and a gust hit. *Orca* leaned abruptly in response, and I held the wheel, keeping her on course. The rush of increased speed made me smile, but it only lasted a moment. Another gust, and this time the wheel bucked a bit. Paul saw my frown and let out the mizzen to relieve pressure on the rudder.

"Afternoon westerlies in the Straits," he offered, and sure enough, south toward Cattle Pass the water was dark navy, salted over with whitecaps that flashed in the afternoon sun. Among the soft hills of the San Juan Islands, the wind was forever changing direction and speed. So far this summer the problem had been too little wind rather than too much.

Then another gust that wasn't a gust, but a freshening wind that stayed. And with it arose the inevitable question: reduce sail now or wait a bit?

It was never an easy decision in conditions like these, when the weather was fair and the sailing spirited, dappled water blurring past the gunwale. We compromised by letting out the main and especially the genoa, which wasn't made for wind much above this, and by making sure the working jib was ready to raise. But the wheel continued to tug at me; *Orca* was resisting my hand at the helm, trying to head up into the wind. Telling me in the plainest terms to slow down.

At first neither of us would listen. Something in the rising wind excites. It pushes against you, and, reflexively, you push back. The faster the wind, the faster you want to go, not just to get to your destination but to meet the challenge that is hitting you, literally, in the face. To reduce sail, or to throttle back if you're motoring, feels like a kind of submission, a giving in, which isn't nearly as thrilling as resistance.

If it hadn't been for weeks of cruising, we might have hesitated when the genoa began to stretch in deep, ugly lines that radiated from the clew to each metal hank on the wire headstay. Instead, we looked at each other, nodded once, and moved to lower it. I pointed the bow right into the wind and switched on the autopilot to keep it there. The main and mizzen, emptied and powerless, rattled their protest. I released the genoa halyard, and Paul, standing on the bowsprit, pulled the sail down, burying half the foredeck in white Dacron.

The effect on *Orca* was immediate. With the genoa down, she lost over half of her driving power. She was almost hove-to, stepping in place, not going forward but not sliding backward either. In the seeming lull Paul raised the working jib, two-thirds the genoa's size, high-cut and heavy. As soon as he secured the halyard, I disengaged the autopilot and turned the wheel to star-board, falling off the wind, filling the sails.

We were almost too late, for the wind soon hard-ened. In another five minutes we would have been struggling with *Orca* as well as the wind, clawing at the genoa to get it down, losing headway and slipping side-ways. Instead, we were charging forward, *Orca* no longer overheeled and oversailed. She moved through the water as she was designed to in twenty knots of wind—efficiently and comfortably. The wheel was easy in my hand.

When the gale-force winds come,
it is always the big tall trees
that get blown over,
while the pliant little grass just
sways back and forth.

BECALMED

We were heading west out the Strait of Juan de Fuca when we saw *Rising Glass* coming our way. The bright yellow kayak strapped to her cabin trunk made her easy to spot from a distance. She seemed to be in as much of a hurry as we were, motoring on a flat, pale blue sea.

As if responding to the same signal, we turned our boats to intersect each other's course. I couldn't remember the last time we'd seen Jim and Sue. *Rising Glass* had been moored in Port Angeles since they'd taken those new teaching jobs; we were still with our same jobs in Seattle. Funny how having a boat didn't necessarily mean we got around a lot. Too bad we were heading in such opposite directions.

Paul put the engine in idle as they approached. I peeled off my sweatshirt—it was hot when we weren't moving.

"Where to?" Jim shouted from *Rising Glass*. He was wearing a T-shirt, but he hadn't shed his cap. He never did. No more than he ever shaved off his red beard and mustache.

"Sequim Bay!" I shouted back. It was one of those anchorages most people bypassed in their rush to the San Juan and Gulf Islands. We'd be there in a couple of hours and envisioned an afternoon lying in the sun, waiting for our crab pots to trap dinner. Maybe do some clamming when the tide went all the way out.

By now Paul had turned *Orca* in the same direction as *Rising Glass*, and we were abeam of each other, Sue dropping fenders over *Rising Glass*'s toerail so we could side-tie for a few minutes. It wasn't a decision; it just happened.

"What about you guys?" I asked as I took their bow-line.

"Mystery Bay," she answered. I knew her eyes were sparkling behind her sunglasses. This was such serendipity, to run into each other on our way to equally delightful harbors in the broad expanse of the Strait of Juan de Fuca. If the strait had been whipped up by westerlies, as it usually was, we would all be sailing, they with the wind, we against it, and the most we would have done on seeing each other was wave.

Paul secured the stern, and Jim suggested a springline "just in case." We were a tidy raft now, three miles from shore, a little closer to our destination than to theirs. Halfway across the strait to the north, Smith

Island was a smudge spiked with a tiny lighthouse, and beyond were the San Juan Islands. Between the mountains on Vancouver Island and the Olympic Peninsula lay the glaring horizon of the strait. Some sixty miles to the west was the ocean, though we seemed to be in a vast lake so still you could canoe across, all the way to Japan. Freighters glided by in the shipping lanes; from a distance they looked like towers or castles, refracted on the glistening, undulating mirror of the sea.

How did it come about that we stayed like that, rafted the entire endless afternoon? Jim adjusted the wheel on *Rising Glass* so she would track with *Orca*. Sue produced a bottle of wine from the galley. At some point I went below and put together a tray of crackers, canned smoked clams, cream cheese, and fruit. Paul and Jim raised *Orca*'s genoa. There was no hint of even the faintest breeze, but somehow the sail filled, holding us in place against the ebb current. So we remained for hours, miles from shore in fifty fathoms of water, our only anchor the unbelievable calm.

It was as if we had discovered a magical, invisible island, a mirage created by the afternoon heat and light that had substance after all.

If we take our time,
we'll achieve what we're seeking
faster than if we hurry.

MAIDEN VOYAGE

For nine months *Ocean Angel* had been tied to the boat-yard pier for refitting. The owners, a California couple in their late fifties, would fly up to Seattle periodically to monitor the progress. Toward the end, Gordon moved aboard, but Lorraine continued to stay home, visiting only now and then. She unapologetically preferred to stay in their comfortable home near San Diego.

"All Gordon wants to do now that he's retired is play with that boat," she complained to me one afternoon, looking back with a grim smile at the sixty-foot power yacht. The deck was crowded with carpenters, electricians, and mechanics, and Gordon seemed to be everywhere at once.

I wasn't surprised that Lorraine was opening up to me this way. Who else was there to talk to? Not the guys working on *Ocean Angel* at forty dollars an hour. Not her husband, apparently, who woke before dawn every morning, drawing up yet another plan for taking his boat yet another step closer to perfection. I was about the only other woman around, and maybe she figured that because I worked on my boat—just then I was kneeling on deck, refinishing the teak caprail—I knew something she didn't about being happy afloat. Or maybe I was just available.

"Is this your first boat?" I asked.

"Oh no," she answered. "When Gordon and I were first married—before the kids came along—we had this runabout we'd take fishing outside San Diego Harbor.

Those were great times. I liked that little boat. But *Angel* is so big. I'll never figure out how she works. And Gordon keeps making her more complicated."

Indeed he did. His GPS, autopilot, radar, depthsounder, weatherfax, and digital chart package would be interfaced so completely, he claimed, that he could cruise the world from his computer screen. Many a night I'd see him up late in the pilothouse, tapping away at the keyboard, working out the bugs.

Lorraine's spirits seemed to rise as she provisioned for the shakedown cruise a month or so later. Gordon had promised that they'd go one place just for fun, and she was determined to be a good sport about all the rest. As if to put her best foot forward, she wore a new foul-weather jacket and new deck shoes when they pulled away.

I wish the weather had been better for her. As is typical in the Pacific Northwest in late June, it rained half the time, or fogged in. Summer never really starts until mid-July; until then the weather tries to improve but can't seem to get it right. At least *Angel* was roomy and comfortable inside.

When they returned, Lorraine was on the bow handling lines—rather skillfully, I thought—but I couldn't read her face.

"How'd it go?" I asked her later that day.

"Just as I expected." She sighed. "Every day Gordon was up at dawn and we had to be under way. He wanted to test all the systems, including the downriggers. He spent one afternoon just trying to get the boat to roll in the strait."

I grimaced over my coffee. "That doesn't sound like much fun."

"It wasn't so bad." She had a tougher stomach than I did, apparently. "I read and went through the charts, not the ones in Gordon's computer—he was always busy on that—but the old paper ones. Some cruising guides too. You know, picking the fun place: Langley."

Good choice, I thought. A protected marina right in town, lots of little shops and galleries and restaurants. More picturesque than a boatyard, for sure.

"But the interesting part was when we left." She leaned over the galley table as if she were going to tell me a secret. "It was early, of course, foggy, could barely make out the shore. We'd been motoring about an hour. And then the electronics went out." Her face brightened, which surprised me; I hadn't thought she was the kind of woman to relish misfortune. "Gordon was real upset. There's usually nothing he can't figure out quickly, but no matter what he did, he couldn't get the screen up. Not the radar, nothing. And the worst part was, he didn't know where we were."

Lorraine paused and took a sip of coffee, savoring her story. Then her words came in an excited rush. "But I did! I'd been following along with the charts—I'd forgotten how I liked doing that—so I wasn't worried at all. I mean, the engine was still working, and the steering. At first Gordon didn't believe me when I pointed to our position, but later, when the fog thinned out a bit, he saw that I was right." She sat back. "We made it down from Possession Point today, with me navigating."

It is not until the external light is extinguished that our internal light shines bright.

LOCKING THROUGH

When the gates opened and the lockmaster announced that he wanted all outbound boats on the north wall, I was running a line from the bow cleat so it would be ready to hand off. I'd already prepared the sternline for Paul, who was at the wheel, keeping enough speed on for steerage, but not so much that he'd have trouble backing down. Reverse gear always crabbed *Orca*'s stern to port, which was tricky when tying up to starboard, as we would have to do in the lock. After more than twenty years of experience, passing from fresh water to salt water and back again, locking through had become

119

routine, an inconvenient necessity we took in stride.

We were second in line, behind a sailboat that appeared to be as heavy and deep-draft as *Orca*. The crew on board handed the lines to the locktenders, who looped the ends on the bollards, though I barely paid attention, busied, as usual, checking our starboard fenders. So I missed whatever it was that went wrong as the crew began to take up the slack in their lines. What I saw was their stern suddenly swing out, their bow nose into the wall, everyone on board scrambling.

"Amateurs," I said to myself without thinking, for we'd never gotten ourselves into that predicament. Paul may have had the same thought; when I glanced at him, he shrugged and throttled down to give them time to straighten out. As we approached the wall, closing the space between our bow and the sailboat's stern, I casually passed the line I'd readied to the locktender, and Paul did the same.

Jeez, but it happened fast! Before either of us could take in the slack, *Orca's* stern swung outward. We'd been parallel, not more than two feet from the wall, and just like that we were a good forty-five degrees out and ten feet away. It was as if we'd been shoved, forcibly, as if water were still rushing from the huge culverts below the surface, as it did when the level was raised—they'd opened the gates before it had settled; we were the second boat in—that had to be it. The explanation came to me instantly, but the solution did not. I ran to the stern to help Paul take in the line, which was impossibly taut. He throttled forward and turned the wheel to bring the stern in; I ran to the bow to take in the slack there, then back to help him do the same with the sternline.

"You're in gear, skipper!" yelled the locktender. Paul

sprang to the helm and reversed just in time. *Orca*'s bowsprit kissed the wall, the bobstay scraped the concrete, and at the last second I jammed a fender between us and the sailboat ahead.

With no room to motor forward, there was nothing to do but straighten *Orca* manually. Paul wrapped the sternline around a winch and cranked while I tailed, holding tension as the line came off the winch. Slowly the stern moved to starboard until we were parallel to the wall. I returned to the bow, and together we muscled *Orca* along, sideways. I pulled up against the taut line with all the strength of my right arm, then pulled in the slack with all the strength of my left, cleating it before I lost what little I had gained. Pull and pull, and finally *Orca* was there, secured.

It seemed to take forever, but it was only a few minutes. As soon as it was over, my right elbow complained, loud and sharp, my hands stung, and my face was damp with sweat. But boats were filling around us, the lock-tender was shouting, and I turned to help the approaching powerboat raft next to us.

In turning I looked up, for just a second. Looking back at me were dozens of people leaning against the fence, locals and tourists watching the ordered chaos of boats locking through. And in their faces—not all of them, but enough—I recognized the expression I'd exchanged with Paul, not five minutes ago, before the rushing water made amateurs of us both.

When you go pointing out
other people's mistakes, the real
error may very well be hidden
in your own misconceptions.

A CRUISING PACE

The little powerboat, stout and upright as a tug, turned into our marina and spun around. Paul was on the dock to take the bowline from Margaret, and I was there to take the sternline from Jack. We still wore the residue of work—Paul in a necktie, just home from the office, and I in my paint-spattered jeans. In contrast, Margaret and Jack, in their loose shirts and baggy shorts, had a far-away look, as if they were scanning the horizon even now, in the city, at the end of their trip.

"Check the feet," Margaret insisted when she stepped aboard *Orca*.

I looked down. Her toenails were dazzling, a deep fire-engine red so shiny the polish looked wet. "Gorgeous," I said. "New color?"

"No," she said, in mock dismay. "Can't you see they're tanned all over?" Sure enough, the strap lines of her sandals were barely visible. "My personal goal for the cruise—accomplished!" And we both laughed at the silliness of it, the wonder of being away for two weeks with nothing more important to do than that.

Jack, who had stayed aboard his boat to jot a few notes in his log, joined the three of us on the aft deck. He brought his chart book, and soon we were retracing their cruise. They'd left Seattle a day later than originally planned—"We couldn't seem to start on time," Margaret said with a shrug—sped north inside Whidbey Island to Penn Cove, and from there harbor-hopped circuitously around the San Juan Islands.

"How was your fuel consumption?" Paul asked. When they'd bought their boat, we figured they'd bomb around from one place to another, full speed, spending in gas what we, in our sailboat, spend in time.

"Depends," Jack answered, and proceeded to explain more than I wanted to know about his experiments with different rpm's in different sea conditions, how he figured distance made good against fuel used, and so on. Jack was the kind of person who could entertain himself for days trying to take the squeak out of windshield wipers; monitoring fuel consumption had been pure pleasure for him. Paul followed every word.

"The short answer is, we did pretty well by going at either twenty-five knots or five," Margaret said. "Fast when it was calm and we had a long distance to go, slow otherwise."

While the guys got increasingly technical, Margaret

pulled out a journal she'd kept, an unlined spiral tablet. Each page was dated, somewhere, but beyond that there was no linear arrangement of events. The pages were filled less with words than with colored-pencil drawings that were outlined and shaded and seemed to flow from one to the other. Cartoonlike, but more real somehow than a photograph, so that a starlit sky seemed to pulsate with light and the reflections in the water seemed to shimmer, the way you remember a night like that, or want to. Even the words were like drawings: there were different lettering styles, at times different colors of letters. Paging through that journal was like seeing with her eyes.

Margaret called her mother to let her know they'd returned. Paul started the barbecue. The four of us improvised a meal. It was a warm evening with an endless blue twilight—the last remaining hours of the last day of their cruise.

That evening was repeated every summer. They'd be out for a couple of weeks, and unless we were out cruising ourselves, on their return they'd stop by, Jack with his log and charts, Margaret with her journal that was like a voyage in itself. The first page was generally full of embellished lists of projects she was up to her neck in, or decisions she was trying to make. She had an architectural business, with all the complexity of permits, contractors, and clients, and a mother in her mid-eighties, in up-and-down health. On that first page, which had little color, she seemed to let those responsibilities go. Then the drawings took over: the hanging flowerpots in Victoria; the clutter on the galley table; Jack asleep, knees up, on the back deck; stones she found on a beach. The lists, when there were any, turned frivolous: favorite words, weather conditions ("wind-calm, water-calm, me-calm"), to-do's ("Eat. Nap. Read. Eat. Row."). And the drawings, too. "You know you're really cruising," Margaret laughed, "when you draw a picture of the cracker you're eating."

They weren't sailors, but they seemed to have found the pace sailors everywhere long for, not by crossing oceans or voyaging for months on end, but by cruising for two weeks in a twenty-seven-foot power-boat. No plans, no schedule. Period. "Think of it this way," explained Jack. "If you don't have any appointments, you're never late." When it turns cool or rainy, head for a town; when it turns rough, change the route or stay put. Tides and currents, daylight and darkness—these, along with pure happenstance, determine the schedule. "We went whale watching and accidentally ended up in Victoria," read one entry, amid blue wavy lines, flowered teacups, and the notes and words to "O Canada."

When it can happen, we are their last stop before reconnecting completely to shore life. They spread their charts and open the journal. Tied to our marina, in the middle of industrial Seattle, we fall, gladly, into their cruise.

Life is being in accordance with
nature, ordinary and not affected.
When you are hungry, eat;
when you are tired, sleep.

DRAGGING ANCHOR

When the squall hit, I stirred in my sleep, but it was something else—a sound—that woke me, completely and instantly. I didn't try to identify it. I didn't roll over and ask Paul what he thought it was. Neither of us spent so much as a second trying to talk the sound away; no "It's OK" or "It's just the chain pulling on the roller." One moment we were asleep, and the next we were up, pulling on jeans and jackets, jamming our feet into shoes. Paul turned the key, and the engine rumbled on.

"We're dragging," he said, though I already knew it, for *Orca* was broadside to the wind, leaning slightly and moving sideways toward shore and shallow water. Somehow the anchor had slipped. A flash of disbelief—this *can't* be happening—and I threw open the hatch and was at the helm, throttling forward, turning the wheel to point into the wind.

Everything was pitched at high volume in the blackness, the rigging screaming, the wind howling, the engine roaring. Paul was hunched over the bow, cranking the windlass; the roller creaked and the pawl clanked and the chain rattled into the locker. I worked the controls and the wheel to hold us into the wind and align the bow with the chain, guided by Paul's gestures to go port or starboard, forward or reverse.

A troller materialized next to us in the darkness. At first it looked like we'd fouled its anchor, but we'd only drifted across its line. By easing forward and sliding the boat along until it was off our stern, we untangled and were free. Paul took a breath and was back on the bow, cranking up the rest of our anchor chain. By this time another boat—a large schooner—had its cabin lights on, its engine running, its crew no doubt awake, though it looked like its anchor was holding.

Unbidden, information reeled from my brain: The bottom in this bay was mud, so if we went aground, the hull wouldn't be damaged. The tide was going out, but it would be back up by midmorning. I remembered a mooring buoy behind the breakwater that had been empty when we turned in the night before; if we got out of this, we could grab it until morning. A little more throttle—that was enough—then reverse; my hands on the wheel and the levers seemed to know how to ease the strain Paul was working against.

From the way his shoulders dropped when he stood up, I knew the anchor was free. Yes, he nodded, joining me in the cockpit, he'd thought of that buoy too. He took the wheel and steered for it while I rigged a bowline. It wasn't easy to snag the buoy with a boat hook and feed the line through the eye in the dark, *Orca* pitching in the chop. It wasn't easy for Paul to find the buoy and hold us there against the wind either.

We didn't shut off the engine right away. We were safe, but pure energy still surged through us; it was only then, in fact, that I became fully aware of my racing heart and breath. We waited a while before going below, a while longer before accepting that we'd be awake all night. We were settling down to a cup of tea and a deck of cards when the wind died so abruptly that it seemed to have been gathered into a box.

Later, as we lay on our backs, trying to sleep, the questions came. Why hadn't the anchor held? We'd done everything to set it well. We'd dragged a couple times before, but never here. We'd never seen the wind come up from the northeast like that in the summer either. True enough, we'd anchored in a slightly different area than usual. Maybe we'd dropped the hook in kelp, or maybe current had corkscrewed the anchor out of an already tenuous hold. Endless maybes.

"It was a good thing you turned on the engine right away," I said.

"Yeah," Paul agreed. "And you at the wheel—you kept the bow right where I needed it."

A silence, and I knew he was thinking, as I was, how we'd never again be sure we were safely hooked, no matter how familiar the harbor. Never be sure that the wind wouldn't pipe up out of nowhere from a direction we hadn't thought possible.

"It's going to be hard next time we anchor."

Paul rolled onto his side, toward me. "But we will, anyway," he whispered. And then he yawned, and then I yawned, and then we slept.

If your mind is like a mirror,
you will be able to respond
automatically to whatever changes
may suddenly occur.

MENDING THE SAIL

"Prepare to come about."

I turned the wheel as Paul released the port sheet and began to pull in on the starboard. Something was wrong; *Orca* wasn't tacking. Paul cleated off the sheet and moved forward to help the genoa around the forestay.

"It's stuck," he yelled from the head of the main mast. "It's that bolt up there I forgot to cover!" He yanked on the luff of the sail, trying to unhook it. I pointed into the wind to ease the pressure and heard a tearing sound, slow and sickening. The sail unhooked and whipped around. I pointed into the wind again. Paul released the halyard, and the genoa billowed down onto the deck.

So much for sailing tomorrow, I thought, as we furled the other sails and motored into the bay. Instead of sipping wine at anchor, watching the blue twilight deepen over the San Juan Islands, we used the dwindling light to examine the damage. The rip was almost a foot long, a ragged slash that paralleled the reinforced luff. *Damn.*

The cause was an easy fix; Paul went aloft the next morning and covered the offending bolt with chafing gear. The repair was another matter. Yes, the sailmaker said on the phone, we could bring the genoa over, but he couldn't get to it right away. Did I still have the sail-mending kit he'd helped me put together years ago? Maybe it was time for me to learn to use it.

I gather up my materials and take a sober look at the work before me. The thing I hate about mending is that it requires as much disassembly as assembly; the area always gets worse before it gets better. Annoyed, I begin cutting and pulling the zigzag stitches off the reinforced hem, then off the hem beneath that. Three rows in all. The morning is warm and still—too nice a day for a chore like this.

"Flatten the area as completely as possible," the sailmaker had said, "and tape down the rip on one side." I tear off a section of wide masking tape and place it sticky side down over the rip. On the back side I adjust the raw edges of the tear so they touch one another, like the lips of a wound ready for suturing. I trim the excess tape with scissors. Down the bay, an outboard starts up. We should be heading out too, not anchored here, but without this genoa we'd get nowhere in such light air. If only Paul had covered that bolt in the first place; it hadn't taken him twenty minutes to do so this morning, after the fact.

"Cut a piece of sailcloth to cover the tear, with seam allowance to spare, but not too much." The raw edges of the patch fray; a quick pass with the flame of a lighter seals them.

"Staple the patch to the sail before you begin sewing." An odd tip, but pins would never penetrate the dense Dacron. The staples make only tiny holes, and hold firmly.

Nice—I almost say it aloud.

I thread the needle, wax the long thread to prevent snarls, and begin the first stitch around the outside of the patch. What I am aiming for are stitches about a quarter-inch long that zigzag around the patch. A machine could do this in a single pass, but sewing it by hand requires slanted stitches one way around (the "zig"), then slanted stitches in the opposite direction (the "zag"), back through the same holes. One small stitch after another, and another, and another. Make each one as perfect as possible, and the whole will be strong and lasting. If the stitches are uneven, the stress won't be distributed equally—some will do all the work, some none at all— and the patch will fail.

You can't rush the job, not if rushing means simply putting on speed. Efficiency comes from a deeper place, an internal metronome that prompts a stepped-up rhythm that suits both you and the work. Push too fast, and you drop stitches, snarl thread, bunch the cloth, fumble the needle. There are only a few elements—your hand, the needle, the thread, the two pieces of cloth— but they must be in balance. When you reach that point, it is like dancing or making music with your fingers.

Mending the sail, I hear the music. How had I forgotten the simple pleasure of handsewing? The tiny pop of the needle as it penetrates the Dacron, the slip of the thread that follows behind it, over and over. Around the patch and back again. Then remove the tape and stitch the edges of the tear to the patch, zigs all around one way, zags all around the other. An hour passes, almost another. I stop to rethread, then pop, slip, pop, slip. A passing skiff sends rolls of water from across the bay, and I roll with *Orca,* with everything aboard. A pair of herons fly low, squawking, their broad wings moving too slowly, it seems, to keep so much bird aloft.

All the zigs and zags anchoring the patch to the sail are complete. One area is out of step with the rest, two stitches where I'd run out of thread and started anew—a small stumble. No matter. Every job should have an imperfection to remind us that we're human. So I've been told, though I've never needed to make a mistake deliberately in order to achieve that. My mistakes happen on their own.

Then the finish, over an hour more, stitching the hem and reinforcing strip. I take a break to keep from rushing. I've enjoyed myself too much, I realize, to end on a frantic note. When I'm done, I run my hand over both sides of the patch. What was ragged is smooth. What was torn is whole. What was weakened is stronger, I know, than ever before.

If performed with care and sincerity,
every little task will resonate
with the truth.

STORM WATCH

The weather service has issued warnings of a "serious storm" this afternoon, with gusts to ninety miles per hour. I know what wind like that means at the dock. Ten years ago, a Thanksgiving Day storm blew ninety-three in Juneau Harbor; the whole sky roared, the rigging thrummed and whined—sounds I could feel as much as hear. In less than an hour our straining lines chafed halfway through. Two years ago, when gusts clocked ninety-one here in Salmon Bay, *Orca* hobby-horsed so violently that the gunwale caught under the dock and splintered the caprail.

Today I've got double lines tied off the bow, the stern, and both springs. I taped old socks around the lines where they rub against the chocks. Extra fenders are in place—big, fat round ones. Every loose object on deck is tied down. I even wired the Charlie Noble so it wouldn't fly off the stove pipe as it did that day in Juneau.

There is nothing to do now but wait.

Waiting, I can almost see the barometer falling. How is it that low pressure, which shouldn't weigh anything, feels so heavy? The bay looks as if it has been pressed flat, and not a bird is flying. My chest is tight.

I watch from the pilothouse as a man on the other dock turns his Chris-Craft around to face the threatened storm, pivoting perfectly in the constricted waterway. Everyone puts out extra line.

Time crawls. The barometer drops another millibar.

1:40 P.M.

After a burst of blinding sunlight, the sky to the south looks bruised. Aloft, the clouds are quickening, but here on the water there is only the barest wind; the tails of the windsock in the rigging are just now fluttering. A seagull seems to slide sideways as it flies inland. Sound distorts: I hear a door slam, the brief blare of a radio, the drone of an engine. My own heart.

I put the teakettle on and listen as the water hums to a boil.

3:00 P.M.

Hard rain, like pebbles on the deck. Then the first howls in the rigging. The wind sock is waving. *Orca* rocks slowly, lines creaking and fittings knocking.

A shudder in the main mast, and a whistling. I put

down the book I have been unable to read. Hail pocks the water and dances on the dock.

A few minutes later the hail turns to rain.

3:30 P.M

Before it happens, it's over. The rain softens, the wind inexplicably dies. The sky is overcast in the ordinary way. The storm extended its paw only to challenge us, then changed its mind.

I am relieved but oddly emptied. I was so prepared this time, for nothing, and I can't seem to uncoil or stop waiting for what has already passed.

A crow calls from the mast, another from a boat across the way. Then half a dozen are tumbling and soaring through the sky. They know what to do when the threat is over.

I put on my jacket and open the hatch. I step off the boat onto the dock. Stretching my arms wide, I walk into the cleansing air.

When something happens,
confront it. When it's over,
empty your mind of it.

A ROWING LESSON

"If you want to row you're going to need a life jacket." Most kids balk when I mention those orange horse collars, but not Mackenzie. She had one over her head, buckled and bowed, before I could get out my next sentence: "And help me bail."

This was the first of many Wednesday afternoons she spent with me the summer she was ten. The two of us had a deal going: she would help me with a household chore, and then we would do something fun.

Mackenzie scooted off the dock and into the inflatable, agile as thought. "Bail with what?" she asked, standing on the floorboards.

"Sit down," I said, easing into the boat. I was going to have to take this a step at a time; it was impossible to get ahead of her. "Keep your weight low so the boat doesn't rock."

She giggled and shifted her weight from foot to foot, creating a little tidal wave of sloshing water inside the inflatable. "You mean like that?" Her brief dance made me laugh—the boat was fairly untippable, all right. And as soon as I laughed she sat down on the seat.

"Use this."—I handed her a plastic bleach bottle cut to serve as a bailer—"I'll use the sponge."

The instant we were done, she flipped the oars into the water.

"Put those back in, Mackenzie," I said. "Paddles toward me." Awkwardly, she returned them to their position, one, then the other. "That's called 'shipping the oars.' You should keep them shipped until you're actually rowing. Good. Now you can undo the line. See how it's wrapped on the cleat?"

"Like an eight!"

"That's right, figure eights crossed over each other. OK, push us away—not that hard—and move to the middle of the seat. Facing me." I was perched on the stern.

Mackenzie sat squarely, her bare feet flat on the floorboards, small hands on the aluminum oars. She shook her blonde hair away from her face and flashed me a smile. I would never get used to her eyes: startling, blue, wide open to take in the world.

I covered her hands with mine. "Just feel what it's like for a while," I said. The oars weren't set in conventional oarlocks, but fixed so that the blades stayed at the proper angle for rowing. This, as much as its stability, made the inflatable a good beginner boat. "Don't fight what I'm doing. Just feel it." Our bodies, linked at the hands, leaned forward, back, forward, back. As we rowed away from the dock, the oars dipped, moved through the water, came up dripping, and dipped again.

"I get it, I get it," she said. "Make the handles move around like I'm cranking something." She wiggled, trying to free her hands, but I held them.

"One more," I said, "but this time we'll use *your* muscles."

"Huh?" At first the boat went nowhere. "Oh! I have to push *and* pull!"

"Exactly." I released her hands, and the boat shot forward. Her next stroke was pretty good, both oars moving more or less the same. Then one oar was up and one down, and when she pulled back, the oar that was up slapped the surface, flipping water over both of us.

"Sorry," she said, eyes dancing.

"Lucky for us it's a nice day," I said, grinning back.

I reached for the oars, but she shook her head. Rightly, for she soon found the rhythm—that synchronous motion of legs, torso, arms, and oars. Sort of.

"Hey! I'm turning!" She twisted around to see where we were going and in doing so dug an oar deeper into the water, turning us even more.

"That's OK," I said. We were out in the channel now, and there was nothing for us to hit. "Go ahead and try turning the other way."

Her face went blank with thought for a moment. "I *can't*," she said, then brightened. "Let's try straight again!"

I put my hands back on hers for a while, ten strokes or so. "Ready to turn?" I asked, and she nodded vigorously. I held one oar up and rowed with the other. Over and over, until I felt Mackenzie's hand take control. "Other way," I said, and we were turning in the opposite direction. "Now straight," and we pulled both oars together, and then she was pulling alone.

Now her movements were more symmetrical, the oars dipping more evenly into the water. Every now and then one oar skimmed the surface; she'd laugh, a brief, unselfconscious kid's laugh, then reposition herself on the seat and try again.

I said nothing. I didn't need to. Watching her, it occurred to me that the fearlessness of girls her age was deeper than bravado, more lasting than innocence. What Mackenzie had, and what I was learning from her, was a lack of fear over making a mistake.

"How'm I supposed to know I'm going straight when I'm sitting backwards?"

Good question. I briefly considered explaining how

to pick a couple of points off the stern and more or less triangulate from that, but I'd lose her interest if I got theoretical. It wasn't important that she learn everything today.

"That comes later," I said. "But here's what I can do now that you know how to turn"—more vigorous nodding on her part—"I'll be your lookout and point the direction you need to go to straighten out."

At first I'd point to starboard, and she'd row with that oar and turn us to port. But she caught on quickly, considering that she had to reverse my hand signals, and was looking backward besides.

"I'm hungry," Mackenzie announced, in the direct way kids announce such things, trusting that action will follow.

"Food's that way," I said, pointing toward shore. "Better turn us around." She did, proudly and swiftly.

By the time we reached the dock, her dad was there, waiting to take her home.

"Did you see me?" she asked excitedly. "I was rowing!"

"Sure did," he said, taking the line I handed him.

"No, Dad!" she shouted as he bent over the dock cleat. "I can do that. Watch." And forgetting all I'd told her about standing up in the boat, moving abruptly to one side, leaving the oars dragging in the water—forgetting it all—she wrapped the line around the cleat in figure eights like an expert.

No teacher can instill a student
with anything; but he can help
that student understand everything
in the student's own mind.

HOME WATERS

Labor Day, and we're stuck in the city. Couldn't get away, and to make it even worse, there's never been a more beautiful Seattle weekend.

I stretch out on a cockpit seat I have entirely to myself, adjusting the pillow behind my back. I don't even have to hold my head up if I don't want to—just rest it on the winch. This isn't so bad. And in just a couple of hours, late in the afternoon, we'll take the boat out.

Out isn't the right word, for what we actually do is take the boat *in*—to Lake Union, to the city. Hardly a remote destination; we could as easily drive or bicycle or walk there. Instead we pull away from the dock and motor up the Ship Canal. At the first bridge we signal—a long and a short—and wait, working the controls to hold position. The traffic on the bridge buzzes like a hive of agitated wasps. Then a deafening blast as the bridge signals an opening, then the clang of dull bells, the creak of gears, and silence as all the cars are stopped and the leaves rise up. We motor through, past the shipyards and marinas, past the flotillas of fishing boats and tugs, past the barges loaded with hills of gravel and sand. The channel narrows to an avenue of poplars. A longer wait at the second bridge, and we're there.

In the middle of Lake Union we cut the engine. Around us floatplanes are landing and taking off at furious, droning intervals, and we joke through our supper of sandwiches and potato salad—it's like having a picnic on an airstrip. But the planes are soon gone, leaving us and a few other boats adrift in this urban landscape, going nowhere.

The wind dies and the lake, glassy now, seems to absorb all the light in the sky as the buildings on shore go into shadow. When does sunset begin? Is it that moment when the city seems to take a deep breath, and hold it? Or is it the moment when a mallard quacks and you suddenly notice the silence? The downtown high-rises, until now dull concrete and vacant glass, turn metallic in the slanted light. The silver, platinum, and chrome towers blaze, then soften to polished bronze or deepen to copper as, unseen, the sun sets far to the west. Long after the rest of the city has lost its color, they hold the light.

A slight, cool breeze signals the arrival of darkness. Running lights on, engine on, we motor back to the dock. The moon rises, huge and orange. Summer is behind us. Fall is ahead. On this night we float between.

You don't need to travel
to some illusory world
to find the principles of life;
just pay attention to the details
of life and experience them.

ACKNOWLEDGMENTS

This book owes much to the work of artist and writer Tsai Chih Chung and translator Brian Bruya. I am equally thankful to writers Sheila Bender, Kip Robinson Greenthal, Christi Killien, and Christine Widman, who generously reviewed my drafts and kept me honest—not just to the facts, but to the underlying spirit. They never let me take the easy route.

Thanks also to my editor, Tom McCarthy, who first launched the idea of this book and then responded to my unexpected proposal with such enthusiasm; and to my agent, Elizabeth Wales.

To all the friends who shared their experiences with me, a special thanks. In most cases I used their real names; but for a few composites, all the stories are true.

Thanks to the Island Institute in Sitka, Alaska, and the Washington Center for the Book in Seattle for giving me time and space to reflect and write.

I write aboard, so I am enormously grateful to the shipwrights at Lake Union Boat Repair, who forwarded my packages and shared their office, their fax machine, and their opinions. Who would have known that struggling with words had so much in common with tearing out dry rot, rebuilding engines, and refinishing teak?

Finally, thanks to my husband, and to the captain and first mate on the good little ship *Jack*. You nitpick when needed, you praise when deserved, making me a better writer. You know my heart.

An earlier version of "Setting Out" appeared in "Only by Boat," *Seattle Times Pacific Magazine* (30 April 1995). An earlier version of "The Right Bait" appeared in *Kinesis* (April 1994).

Aphorisms on pages 20, 23, 28, and 101 are reprinted from *The Dao of Zhuangzi: The Harmony of Nature,* by Tsai Chih Chung. Copyright © 1997 by Tsai Chih Chung. Trans. © 1997 by Brian Bruya. Used by permission of Doubleday, a division of Random House, Inc.

Aphorisms on pages 8, 46, 85, and 107 are reprinted from *The Tao Speaks: Lao-Tzu's Whispers of Wisdom,* by Tsai Chih Chung. Translated by Brian Bruya. Copyright © 1995 by Tsai

LIST OF MESSAGES

ABOUT THE AUTHOR

Seattle-based author Migael Scherer has been cruising the waters of the Pacific Northwest and living aboard since 1974, when she and her husband launched the sailboat they had spent two years building. Her cruising experience includes four years in Southeast Alaska and three trips on the fifteen-hundred-mile Inside Passage. Her first book, *Still Loved by the Sun: A Rape Survivor's Journal* (1992), won a PEN/Albrand citation for distinguished nonfiction and a Pacific Northwest Booksellers Award. She is author of numerous magazine articles and of the oft-praised *A Cruising Guide to Puget Sound* (International Marine, 1995).